Gardeners'
Worldmagazine

101 Ideas for
Small Gardens

10 9 8 7 6 5 4 3 2 1

Published in 2009 by BBC Books,
an imprint of Ebury Publishing
A Random House Group Company

Copyright © Woodlands Books Limited 2009
Words by Martyn Cox
All photographs © Gardeners' World Magazine

The Random House Group Limited Reg. No. 954009

Addresses for companies within the Random House Group can be
found at www.randomhouse.co.uk

A CIP catalogue record for this book is available from the British Library.

ISBN 9781846077319

The Random House Group Limited supports The Forest Stewardship
Council (FSC), the leading international forest certification organization.
All our titles that are printed on Greenpeace approved FSC certified
paper carry the FSC logo. Our paper procurement policy can be found
at www.rbooks.co.uk/environment

Commissioning editor: Lorna Russell
Project editor: Helena Caldon
Designer: Kathryn Gammon
Picture researcher: Janet Johnson
Production controller: David Brimble

Colour origination by: Dot Gradations Ltd
Printed and bound in Germany by Firmengruppe APPL,
aprinta druck, Wemding

Gardeners' World magazine

101 Ideas for Small Gardens
BRILLIANT WAYS TO CREATE BEAUTIFUL SPACES

Author
Martyn Cox

Contents

Introduction

Ask the owner of a large garden if they'd consider swapping their plot for one the fraction of the size and I doubt if they are likely to say 'yes'. For these gardeners, the thought of trading in a sweeping lawn, substantial borders and a generous water feature for a space the size of a postage stamp is enough to bring on a cold sweat.

But size really isn't everything. It is perfectly possible to create an exciting, attractive, functional, and plant-filled space even if you can step out of the back door of your house and almost touch the rear wall of your garden with an outstretched arm.

For proof, look no further than this book. Inside you will find 101 ideas that will inspire and help you create the small garden of your dreams. Divided into six sections, you'll find planting and tips to make the most of every nook, cranny, gap, fissure, structure and surface in the garden. There's even advice on how to maintain and keep the garden going once you've built it.

So don't feel hamstrung by your tiny plot. With a little bit of imagination, creativity and this book, you will soon have a garden to be proud of.

Martyn Cox
Gardeners' World Magazine

Boxing clever

Disguise bare stems with neatly manicured box.

Time to plant: Spring or autumn.

Most of us wouldn't dream of going outside without our socks on unless it was a blazing hot day, so why should it be any different for trees? This slender trunk would look a little vulnerable and cold without a neatly manicured cube of box (*Buxus sempervirens*) around its naked ankles.

Perfectly suited to a formal, minimalist garden, the geometric shape of the box echoes other features in the garden, such as nearby garden furniture. Its neat lines mirror the square pattern of the paving material – the vibrant green contrasts brilliantly with the dazzling white stone.

A uniform block of box like this would jar if planted under a tree that is allowed to grow naturally with minimal interference from a pair of secateurs. However, here it is perfectly placed under an architectural tree, whose neatly clipped head sits on top of a long length of bare stem. Sometimes the crown of these trees can seem to 'float' as the stems are so lean, but planting at the base helps to ground it and draw it back into the design.

TIP
To keep your topiary sharp, prune box in mid-June, when the leaves are hard and leathery, and again in late summer, if necessary. For accuracy, prune with a pair of hand-held clippers, such as sheep shears.

Leading lines

A series of containers can link one part of the garden to another.

Time to plant: Spring or autumn.

Metallic clumps of astelia, an architectural plant that originates from Australia, make a strong statement rising from tapered containers. The silvery, strap-shaped leaves sparkle in sunshine and contrast vividly with the dark tones of the pot.

A single container planted with an astelia would make an eye-catching feature, but here they become a design tool. A number of plants grown in identical containers can be used to add movement to a space, leading the eye from one part of the garden to another. For instance, they could be placed up a flight of steps, along a low wall or down a path. Choose containers that complement the plants you are planning to grow and are large enough to accommodate their rootballs.

A series of containers like this can also be placed in a row to create a visual and physical barrier alongside a patio, or to separate off one part of the garden.

TIPS
Cover the surface of the compost with a mulch of decorative gravel to suppress weeds and reduce moisture loss. Raise containers on pot feet over winter to help water drain away.

Break it up

Divide up your garden to add interest.

Time to do it: Spring or autumn.

Some garden owners despair of their small rectangular plot and largely lay it to lawn, but by dividing it up you can create a much more stimulating space. Partitioning the garden allows you to enjoy several styles and different types of plants, while creating visual movement. It also entices you to physically move from one part of the garden to another.

Here, the garden has been broken up into four visually defined areas that link together. A patio near the house with stone paving makes the perfect place to sit out and leads to a pergola that rises before a sea of gravel – the change of surfacing material indicates a change of zone. A formal lawn leads to a natural area, where a pond and a mixture of ornamental and native plants attract wildlife.

TIPS
Don't try to squeeze in too many zones – allow each to 'breathe' for the best effect. Hide some areas with trellis, hedges or tall plants so you don't see the garden in its entirety.

Spark up shady corners

Plant groups of hostas to brighten up the gloom.

Time to plant: Spring or autumn.

In a small garden it's likely that you'll have pockets of shade created by neighbouring buildings, trees or the planting in your own garden. Rather than curse these gloomy spots and leave them vacant, look on it as an opportunity to grow plants that thrive in limited light.

If your patio doesn't get much sun, brighten it up with a group of hostas in pots. These plants thrive in shade, rewarding you with large, textured leaves, plus lavender-coloured flowers in summer. Protect hostas from slugs by sticking a band of copper tape around each pot.

Choosing a selection of different hostas is a great way to play around with colour, but just a single variety, especially if it has golden or lightly variegated foliage, will really brighten up the gloom. Plant your hostas in different-sized pots to give the display greater impact.

TIPS
Group pots in odd numbers for a balanced display. Alternatives to hostas include busy Lizzies (*Impatiens walleriana*), sweet flag (*Acorus gramineus*) and several types of sedge, (such as *Carex comans* 'Frosted Curls' and *C. phyllocephala* 'Sparkler'), which are equally good in pots in a shady spot.

New fillings

Turn a gravelled area into an attractive feature.

Time to do it: Any time of year.

Gravel is extremely cost-effective, as it has so many uses in the garden. It can be turned into a cheap and cheerful surface for paths and driveways, be spread thickly as a mulch between drought-tolerant plants, or used to fill any awkward gaps at the edges of patios or paths. Many people even use gravel as a quick fix for parts of the garden that they haven't got around to deciding what to do with, spreading it across a large area.

While it is functional, a sea of stones lacks any eyecatching features. A copious sweep of gravel is unlikely to have any visitors to your garden gasping in awe. However, it is easy to pep it up – simply mix in some glass chippings that have been tumbled to remove any dangerous edges. These are available in many single colours or can be bought in mixed bags.

TIP
For a textural look, choose tumbled glass pieces that are a different size to your gravel – they are generally available in pieces measuring between 3mm and 18mm.

Winding, wonderous walkways

Let curving paths add mystery to the garden.

Time to do it: Any time of year.

Paths are not just a functional way to get from A to B, they can take you on an exciting and mysterious journey, making the garden a more interesting place to explore.

Unless you want a minimalist or ultra-formal garden, it's best to avoid straight paths, as these allow you to see too much of the garden in one go and force you to create uniform beds for planting. A curved path partially obscures the view ahead, enticing you forward, while being more suitable for a relaxed planting scheme.

In this garden, stepping stones have been set into a grass path that bisects well-planted borders. The combination of materials create a striking visual effect, but it also has a practical purpose – the stepping stones ensure you can walk around the garden in all weathers without getting your feet wet and dirty.

TIPS
Ensure your path has adequate foundations and is wide enough to walk down comfortably with a wheelbarrow. Paths look best if made from materials that are similar in colour or style to those used on your house.

Make a splash in a small space

Space-saving ways with water.

Time to do it: Any time of year.

A powerful jet of water splashes against the inside of a glass ball in this contemporary water feature. Ideal for the tiniest of gardens, water features such as this are easy to build and are a perfect way to bring the relaxing sight and sound of water into your garden.

When you're really short on space, even the smallest pond will take up far too much room. However, a water feature is a much more viable option; whether it's a modern design, a barrel fountain, a pebble fountain or a bubbling urn.

This glass ball would be excellent positioned at the side of a patio, at the foot of a wall, or to add interest to a shady corner where nothing seems to grow.

TIP
Water features need an outdoor electricity supply – if you don't already have a socket, employ a qualified electrician to install one for you.

Green up a gloomy garden

How to have a lush lawn, even in a shady spot.

Time to do it: Spring and autumn.

If you have a particularly shady garden, your first question should be whether it is worth creating a lawn or not. Most of us like the idea of a verdant sward, but deprived of light a carpet of green will grow poorly and can soon turn into a muddy patch largely populated by weeds and moss.

However, establishing a lawn in shade is not impossible. Rather than pick normal domestic turf (that needs about four hours of light a day to look good), choose turf that has been created specifically to thrive in shade. If you want to start a lawn from seed, buy a mix containing grasses that will do well in low light. These comprise a high percentage of fine-leaved grasses, including creeping red fescue and smooth-stalked meadow grass.

TIPS
The key to caring for a shady lawn is to cut it less frequently and allow the grass to grow a little longer. An alternative for very shady areas is fake grass – it comes in many styles and colours, and is even available in a variety of piles, just like a carpet.

Lighten up

Use plants to break up expanses of hard landscaping.

Time to plant: Spring and autumn.

This tiled path makes an attractive and durable surface to walk on, but imagine it without any plants. The combination of this and the expanse of gravel next to it would leave a sea of hard paving materials that would be extremely harsh on the eye.

However, add a few plants and the stark scene is immediately softened. In this garden, the designer has not completely paved the path, but has left a few spaces for plants. The rounded shape of the neatly clipped balls of box make a pleasing contrast to the square tiles, and they help to break up the hard edges of the path.

On the opposite side of the path, the feathery pink plumes of pennisetum provide a splash of colour and their relaxed style of growth adds a touch of informality to a fairly formal space.

TIP
The minimal use of plants to soften hard landscaping, as seen here, suits a modern, low-maintenance garden. If you have a less formal space, don't be afraid to really mask the edges of paths with lots of plants.

Coping with slopes

Get to grips with a steep incline by dividing it into levels.

Time to do it: Any time of year.

There's no doubt that sloping gardens are more challenging to design than flat ones. Some people will admit defeat with such a space and decide to leave it exactly as it is. They'll continue struggling to carry tools up and down the slope or burning off far too many calories pushing a mower across a lawn on a steep incline.

But it doesn't have to be this way. Yes, slopes are tricky, but it's possible to tame them by dividing them into a series of horizontal levels. To do this you'll need to design the garden using a combination of terraces, sloping paths, steps, raised beds and retaining walls. (Unless you're really handy at DIY, this sort of construction work is probably a job for the professionals.)

In this tiny garden, a mixture of materials, such as timber or stone for walls, creates visual interest. Room has even been found for a lawn, and its compact size and even level make it easy to care for.

TIP
Make terraces as generous as possible – too many small level areas with lots of steps connecting them will make the garden seem smaller.

Raise it up

Feel the therapeutic effect of a small raised pond.

Time to do it: Any time of year.

A raised pond is the perfect way to turn a courtyard or patio garden into your own private oasis. On a blazing hot day the surface sparkles magically, while the sound of water gently trickling into the pond will help you to relax and forget your cares. It will also partially disguise any noise coming from beyond your garden.

Most raised ponds are formal in design and suit being placed next to a wall or fence, unless access is needed all the way around. Give them a broad rim and you can increase the amount of seating space in your garden – nothing is better than sitting on the side of a raised pond, running your fingers through the water.

Apart from their visual appeal and calming effect, ponds offer plant-mad gardeners a chance to grow specimens that can't be grown anywhere else, such as dwarf water lilies.

TIPS
Site your pond in a slightly shaded spot to reduce the build-up of algae. Plant it up using a mix of submerged oxygenators, marginals and floating aquatics.

Life's a beach

An easy-care surface for the time-starved gardener.

Time to do it: Any time of year.

Are you always at work, or have far too many commitments that prevent you gardening as often as you'd like? If the answer is yes, yes, and yes, but you still want a beautiful garden, make life easy for yourself by creating a low-maintenance space that will largely take care of itself.

In this garden, the owner has ensured no time is spent mowing a lawn, sweeping a patio, or weeding, by covering the entire area with gravel over weed-suppressant matting. This has been combined with large slate paddle stones in places, so the surface doesn't get too boring. All this needs in order to remain attractive all year is the occasional levelling with a rake.

The owners have also spared themselves work by choosing plants that rarely need watering, such as this handsome olive tree. The purple aeoniums beneath have been plunged through the gravel and matting for the summer.

TIP
To save yourself more work, install an automatic watering system to ensure plants in pots get adequate moisture.

Perk up your patio

A quick solution for a tired paved area.

Time to do it: Any time of year.

Removing the odd slab from a patio is the perfect way to create planting pockets. However, this is only a practical option if the paving is loose, otherwise it's near impossible to do without making a real mess.

The solution? Well, you can forget about hacking away at the mortar with a bolster chisel and mallet – all you need to do is make a temporary display using plants in containers. Plant pots for seasonal interest by choosing bulbs or annuals to suit your chosen colour scheme. Here, tall-growing iris grows up behind the pots, adding an extra tier of flowers.

A group of attractive pots arranged tastefully in several areas of the patio helps to break up a monotonous surface. It'll look even better if you surround the pots with different grades of pebble to provide a textural look. Here, ground-covering alyssum in tiny pots have been set among the stones to add more interest at ground level. Further back, a shady spot near the house is perfect for these hostas, whose flower colour matches the timber staining

TIPS
Evergreen plants will provide year-round interest, but include some perennials or annuals that can be changed for new ones once their floral show is over. Arrange the pebbles carefully so the effect looks natural and not too staged.

Pots of impact

Display decorative items to great effect.

Time to do it: Any time of year.

A garden is not only about plants. Adding ornaments is a great way to express your personality in the space or show off a collection of treasures in an outdoor setting. It also allows you to put the finishing touches to a garden – a bit like adding polished steel-light switches once a room has been decorated.

While some ornaments, such as classical figurines or a modern sculpture, are perfect as a focal point to attract the eye, they can also be used in a more subtle manner. For instance, this curvaceous urn, which will develop a wonderful patina as it ages gracefully, has been placed among the foliage of euphorbias, plume poppy and *Cercis canadensis* 'Forest Pansy'. Semi-hidden, it will provide a welcome surprise to all those who venture through the garden.

TIP
Choose ornaments that suit the style of your garden. You don't have to spend lots of money – try recycling junk found in skips. But don't overdo it – too many ornaments in a small space will create a chaotic effect.

Stepping up

Perk up a boring path.

Time to do it: Any time of year.

When you think of a space with an imaginative layout, strong structure and lots of plants bursting with health, the gardens laid out around new-build homes don't immediately spring to mind. Many have been designed simply to help sell the property and it is up to the owner to embellish the garden they have acquired.

Among the features you might find in one of these gardens is a cheap and cheerful gravel path. Rather than live with this expanse of tiny pebbles or chippings, why not give it a facelift?

A few good-quality stone slabs can be placed into the path to break up the monotonous effect created by the gravel. Go for stones whose colour and texture contrast with that of the pebbles. A few plants dotted into the gravel will help soften the look of these hard materials. Provide temporary colour by moving plants in pots on to the path when they are in flower, such as the vibrant daylily used here.

TIP
Choose hard-wearing, spreading plants for your path, such as thymes, *Euphorbia myrsinites*, lady's mantle (*Alchemilla mollis*), prostrate rosemary and houseleeks. Allow plants to grow over the slabs to mask the harsh edges.

Geometry lesson

Simple structural design.

Time to do it: Any time of year.

Informal gardens with a fairly loose structure have their place, but it's much easier to maintain and plant a garden that has been designed with a strong, formal backbone. In this small town garden the space has been divided up with a number of interlocking squares and rectangles, resulting in a series of 'rooms' that lead one to another.

Such a geometric garden could be tough on the eye, but the hard edges of the design have been softened by the planting scheme. A neat lawn surrounds a clipped bay cone, which acts as both focal point and living sculpture. Low bedding surrounding this allows seasonal changes to be made very easily, adding a colourful carpet to the display.

Behind, a band of planting helps to break the view into the rest of the garden. Apple trees add vertical interest, while a screen of airy *Verbena bonariensis* provides some privacy for anyone wanting to sit out under the pergola.

TIPS

Unless you want a contemporary, formal look, allow plants next to paths to spread out and soften the hard lines. Grow plenty of evergreens to provide year-round interest.

Rills of reflection

A compact canal to delight the senses.

Time to do it: Any time of year.

A rill is a classic water feature that is used to visually and physically link different water features or several parts of a garden. Essentially a formal, narrow canal, a rill is often seen running down the centre of long, linear spaces.

In a really small garden, a traditional rill set into the ground would be an inconvenience, but here it has been given a modern twist. Raised up to the top level of the terrace, this rill has been built to one side, where it won't get in the way of people wandering about the garden and allows the owners to fully utilise the floor space.

Gently flowing through a lush tapestry of irises, lady's mantle (*Alchemilla mollis*), aquilegias and clumps of pink-flowered persicaria, the rill is a delight for the senses. Reflective water is a visual treat and its sound has a very calming effect on all those in the garden, while masking any unwanted outside noise.

TIP
Use materials that suit the style of your garden. Reflective, metallic or stone rills look great in a modern urban setting, but might jar in a rural space, where a brick-lined rill may be more appropriate.

Backyard oasis

How to plant a private paradise.

Time to do it: Spring and autumn.

This garden dispels the myth that you can't grow lots of plants in a small garden. By filling it with all their favourites, the owners have managed to create a private and secret retreat.

Growing so many plants in close proximity has given this space a jungle-like feel, but despite being crammed to the gunnels it doesn't feel disorganised.

When planting for impact, aim to achieve a layered look. Put larger trees and shrubs around the boundary, followed by medium-sized shrubs and perennials, then shorter plants at the front. To ensure the garden remains interesting all year round, include some evergreens and underplant with bulbs to give splashes of colour in spring, summer and autumn.

TIPS
To ensure larger plants don't get out of hand, remove unwanted branches. Train climbers into trees so they really earn their keep. Dense planting with trees and tall shrubs creates shade, so leave some areas free for sun-loving plants.

No garden? No problem

Make the most of what you've got.

Time to plant: Spring and autumn.

You don't need a conventional garden to grow lots of plants. There's not a scrap of soil to be seen on the outside of this mews house, but the owners still manage to grow more plants than you'd find in many small gardens.

Everything is grown in pots, and choosing a wide range of different shapes and sizes helps to create a multi-layered, 3D effect. Height at ground level is provided by a birch tree in a container, which is underplanted to make the most of the available space.

Vertical surfaces play an important part in this garden. Window boxes have been placed on the sills of the upper floors, allowing trailing foliage plants to cascade down the bare walls. A tender parlour palm adds an exotic touch, its fronds arching out from inside the house to caress the balcony railings.

As with all container collections, special attention must be given to regular watering through summer and any dry periods. Also remember that plants growing in compost require regular feeding.

TIP
Take the strain out of daily watering by setting up an automatic trickle watering system.

Divide and conquer

Make a practical and comfortable outdoor dining area.

Time to do it: Any time of year.

In the summer, cooking and eating outdoors is one of life's greatest pleasures. But for an al fresco meal to be a complete success, you need to give some thought to the design of your garden. Nobody likes to be suffocated by the fumes from a barbecue when they eat, so if possible you need to separate the cooking and dining areas.

In a large garden it's easy to keep the two apart, but in a small space you need to use cunning. One option is to divide the garden using different levels. A cooking area would naturally suit being near the house, so you can easily grab ingredients or wash tools, while a raised area at the back would be far enough away from the barbecue to be the perfect outdoor dining room.

TIP

For comfortable outdoor eating, ensure your dining area has plenty of shade – either make use of nearby trees or put up a shade sail or parasol.

Putting the fun in functional

Give a dull surface a facelift.

Time to do it: Any time of year.

A stone or slab path is functional, hardwearing and fairly straightforward to build, but, let's face it, it's not very exciting. You see your paths every time you look out of the window or step into the garden, so why not create something that's kinder on the eye?

A path made from log rings is easy to lay and has bags of character, making a tactile surface that you won't be able to resist walking on with bare feet. Because it's made of a natural material, it's perfectly suited to a country or woodland garden. However, it looks equally good in a contemporary, urban space, where it can be combined with pebbles and gravel in a seaside or drought-tolerant planting scheme.

TIPS

When using log rings, don't make a straight path, as the material suits a curvaceous, serpentine design. You can buy log rings from saw mills, woodland timber specialists, or online. Choose different shapes and sizes for a textured path.

Spring into summer

Long-lasting container display.

Time to plant: Autumn.

The key to any good container planting, especially when you may only have room for one or two pots, is to ensure it looks good for as long as possible. Plant it so there is a succession of interest.

Who could fail to swoon at this dark and desirable combination that provides a year-round show in the garden? Overflowing the edges of the pot is a sea of scalloped-leaved heucheras, an evergreen perennial prized for its gorgeous foliage. Above these rise the globular heads of a purple tulip perched on slender stalks.

After the spring blooms start to fade, the heucheras continue to hold your attention, their dramatic foliage perfectly complementing the pink shade of the pot. Tidy up the heuchera by removing damaged leaves in spring. During late spring and early summer, the eye is drawn from the foliage to a mass of short stalks holding dainty, red, bell-like flowers.

TIP
Tulip bulbs are best planted in November. After the tulips go over, you can remove them and replant with a different colour in the autumn.

Learning to share

Making the best use of containers.

Time to plant: Spring or autumn.

When you have lots of space, you can give plants in pots plenty of elbow room to spread out. However, when things are tight you have to make the most of every spare inch.

Olive trees (*Olea europaea*) are classic plants for a wooden Versailles container, but in this small garden there isn't enough space to allow a single plant to take centre stage. Instead, the olive has been planted to one side, which has allowed a rosemary (*Rosmarinus officinalis*) to be squeezed in. Tumbling over the sides is *Euphorbia myrsinites*, a prostrate species that has trailing stems clothed with rounded, glaucous leaves.

This combination of plants is ideal for a sunny spot. It would also suit anyone who is pushed for time, as all the plants are drought tolerant, so will only need occasional watering.

TIPS

These plants love well-drained, gritty compost. Low-maintenance doesn't mean no maintenance, and you will have to prune them to keep them within bounds. Water the container occasionally, especially in hot weather.

Summer sojourn

Exotic ways with tender plants.

Time to plant: Spring.

So you think houseplants can only be grown indoors? Well, think again. With a little imagination it's easy to create some amazing displays with these tender plants, which can grace the garden from late spring until the end of summer.

For an exotic spectacle, plant mother-in-law's tongue (*Sansevieria trifasciata* var. *laurentii*), which has thick, bolt-upright, succulent leaves at the back of a large pot and then arrange two asparagus ferns (*Asparagus densiflorus*) either side of it. Fill the gaps with spider plants (*Chlorophytum comosum* 'Vittatum') and variegated tradescantia, whose stems should be allowed to cascade down the sides of the pot.

Most houseplants are also easy to propagate, and some of these are no exception. Spider plants produce arching stems carrying new 'baby' plants at their tips. Once large enough, these can be removed and potted up to produce new plants. Trailing tradescantia stems about 15cm (6in) long can be removed and rooted in a jam jar of water.

Well what are you waiting for? Liberate your houseplants from a dusty windowsill and give them a summer holiday outdoors.

TIPS

Put the container in a frost-free place over winter. Houseplants will grow quickly in sunshine, so water regularly. Lift and divide spider plants when they have outgrown their allotted space.

Plugging gaps with pots

Drop plants in containers into borders to fill bare patches.

Time to plant: Spring and summer.

These pineapple lilies (*Eucomis*) look like they are romping away in this leafy border. However, these South African bulbs are sun-loving plants that are more likely to sulk if they were planted in such a shady position.

In fact, the pineapple lilies, which have a stout flower spike topped with a tuft of green leaves, were grown in pots in a sunnier part of the garden. Then, when they came into flower, they were added to this bed to give it a boost.

This is an ideal way to fill bare patches in the bed. You don't need to dig a hole to plunge the pot into – simply disguise it with leaves from a neighbouring plant. This is easier to do if you grow the bulbs in black containers, rather than brightly coloured ones that will stand out like a sore thumb.

TIPS
Cannas, dahlias, gladioli, lilies and other sun-loving bulbs in pots make excellent gap fillers. Keep the pots well watered for a long-lasting display. If putting sun-loving plants into a shady spot, make sure they are in flower or about to flower when you do so.

Cover up

Use houseplants to mask an ugly feature.

Time to plant: Spring to early autumn.

You either love or hate brightly coloured *Begonia rex*. Some see them as dust-gathering houseplants that were at their height of popularity during the 1970s, while others love them for their splash of tropical colour.

Whatever you think of them, their huge leaves and spreading habit means they are excellent plants for disguising drains, water butts, broken bits of wall or anything else unsightly in the garden.

The best way to do this is to create a display with them around the offending feature. Leave them in their pots and arrange them with other houseplants, such as coleus and spider plants, along with annual flowers and perennial grasses. For a 3D effect, and to add vertical interest, raise some plants on upturned plant pots.

TIPS
Aim to hide the pots at the front of this temporary display with trailing plants or plants placed on their side. Replace plants often for an ever-changing spectacle. Houseplants will grow quickly outside and need repotting.

Shady couple

A lush combination to brighten up a gloomy spot.

Time to plant: Spring or autumn.

There may be a tendency to curse shady spots in the garden, but rather than let them get you down, look on them as an opportunity to grow plants that will thrive in low light.

Many shade-loving plants will provide your garden with a lush, leafy feel. Perhaps the best plants for these tricky areas are ferns and there are heaps you can choose from, such as this handsome *Polystichum tsussimense*.

Commonly known as the Korean rock fern, *Polystichum tsussimense* forms dense clumps of dark green foliage, eventually growing up to 40cm (16in). Its lance-shaped fronds contrast well with the oval, speckled leaves of *Pulmonaria officinalis*. During spring, this verdant twosome is given a colourful lift, when flower shoots rise from the pulmonaria, carrying small pink blooms that turn to violet and blue as they age.

TIPS

Divide congested clumps of pulmonaria every few years in spring or autumn. *Pulmonaria officinalis*, or Jerusalem cowslip, is a versatile plant, as it can also be grown in full sun.

Bursting with life

Make the most of a dry-stone wall.

Time to plant: Spring or autumn.

Dry-stone walls, whether they surround your garden, divide it up, or retain a raised bed, are often overlooked as a planting space. However, the chinks and gaps between stones on the vertical face of the wall are ideal for filling with small, compact plants, such as ferns, alpines, herbs and hardy succulents.

Wide, deep gaps are the easiest to plant up, as there should be plenty of room to squeeze in a good handful of gritty compost. Next, make a hole in the compost and push your chosen plant firmly in, ensuring the roots are well covered. Finish by using a hand-held sprayer to dampen the compost.

Once established, the plants should grow quickly, and hopefully some will self-seed into othe gaps to give the wall a natural look.

TIPS
Grow plants in John Innes No.2 compost. Suitable plants include houseleeks (*Sempervivum*), *Erigeron karvinskianus*, saxifrages, lewesias, corydalis, sedums and wild strawberries.

Winning rosettes

Tiny plants that are big on looks.

Time to plant: Any time of year.

Native to mountainous regions of Europe, houseleeks, or sempervivums, are the perfect plants for small gardens. They will root absolutely anywhere and are ideal for planting in tiny gaps on the tops and sides of walls, between paving slabs or in rock gardens.

A novel way to grow them is to make a brick planter. To do this, take an old engineering brick (those with three holes down the centre) and fill each channel with a gritty compost mix. You will now need three rosettes of sempervivums – simply divide up a clump, ensuring that each rosette has a length of stem and some roots. Finally, make a small hole in each bit of compost and push the stem in.

The plants will soon root and spread across the surface of the brick. Use it as a moveable feature – it looks great as the centre of an outdoor table decoration.

TIPS
Choosing houseleeks isn't easy – there are more than 1000 different types, in a rainbow of colours, with rosettes that range in size from 5–20cm (2–8in). Houseleeks like to grow in a sunny place in the garden and don't need extra watering once they are established.

Less is more

Keeping colour in the border simple.

Time to plant: Spring or autumn.

Unless you are a plant collector with no self-control over your wallet or over your urge to snap up every specimen that takes your fancy, it is best to show some restraint when planting up a border.

A collection of plants has its place, and for plant lovers a garden is like an outdoor museum where they can exhibit and store their treasures. However, the cumulative effect of so many different colours, shapes, sizes and types of plants crammed in cheek by jowl can sometimes jar.

Far easier on the eye is to plant a border using a limited colour scheme. Here, a tapestry of mainly yellow perennials is occasionally broken by a splash of purple from some dramatically dark irises.

TIP
Use accent colours frugally or they will end up dominating a display – dot them into the border irregularly for a natural-looking effect.

Potted colour

Foliage plants and bright pots for a quick colour fix.

Time to plant: Sow seeds in early spring. Buy ready-grown plants in late spring.

Does your garden look a little dull? Then give it a shot in the arm by injecting some quick colour. While there are many flowering annuals or pot plants you could choose, why not try something different with some fantastic foliage plants, such as oxalis, ipomoea and plectranthus? These can be grown in pots, hanging baskets, window boxes or troughs.

Perhaps the most exuberant of all are coleus (*Solenostemon scutellarioides*). A few years ago these leafy plants were considered passé, but they are now much more widely grown. They are available in a range of vibrant colours, including reds, oranges, yellows, greens and pinks, along with combinations of several of these shades. The 'Kong' series are particularly showy – these 55cm (22in) tall plants have leaves that are 30cm (12in) long.

For maximum impact, grow these colourful beauties in a selection of bright, glazed ceramic pots.

TIPS
Although generally grown as annuals, coleus can be kept going all year round if moved to a frost-free place over winter. Remove any flowers and pinch back the tips regularly for bushy plants.

Grape pretender

A clever way to grow grape hyacinths.

Time to plant: Bulbs in autumn.

At first glance you could be forgiven for thinking that a new variety of grape hyacinth (muscari) had been discovered with flowering stems twice as big as normal. But take a closer look…

There's nothing unusual about this grape hyacinth. It's the traditional, well-loved, spring-flowering type whose tiny heads of blue flowers bear a passing resemblance to Marge Simpson's hairdo. However, it has been grown in a rather unusual way.

At only 15cm (6in) tall, these flowers are easily lost, even in a small garden, so to make an impact with them you need to be creative. One way of doing this is to pile compost up in a large container to make a pyramid shape. Then cover it with a fine grade of chicken wire. Now all you have to do is plant bulbs through the holes, sit back and wait for a sensational spring display.

TIP
Plant bulbs about 7.5cm (3in) deep. Place the container in a sunny position and really enjoy the flowers by raising the pot up on a garden bench or table, which won't be used so early in the year.

Green scene

Create the perfect backdrop for spring and summer colour.

Time to plant: Spring or autumn.

The horizontal branches of a wedding cake tree (*Cornus controversa* 'Variegata') embrace a border in mid-spring. At this time of year the display is cool and lush, a mass of fresh hues of green that give the space a calming look. Walking into a garden that is full of limes, emeralds, jades and zesty spring greens is instantly relaxing and an excellent antidote to the stresses of a busy day.

However, this is a garden on the cusp. Within weeks the verdant tapestry will provide the perfect foil for an explosion of colour. The perennials that have been crammed into the bed burst into flower – walk into the garden and it will invigorate you. Elsewhere, the changing of the seasons is celebrated on the patio, where large terracotta pots have been generously planted with lilies, whose towering flower stems will hold huge vibrant flowers.

TIPS

Plant lily bulbs in spring. When planting lots of perennials, add a few evergreen shrubs at the back of the border to give year-round interest. Underplant a perennial border with spring and autumn bulbs to give splashes of colour.

Dare to be different

A hot and fiery show of exotics.

Time to plant: Spring.

Design rules would suggest that it is best to avoid a tropical show of hot and fiery clashing colours in a small garden. It's much safer to go for a limited colour scheme. Lots of different plants in many jazzy shades can be painful on the eye. It can look clumsy and can make a small garden seem even smaller.

However, creating a garden is all about personal taste, and if you're bored by muted tones and fancy a border stuffed with architectural plants and loud perennials, just go for it. Rising up at the back of this vibrant border are castor oil plants (*Ricinus communis*), which loom above red, yellow and purple dahlias. Splashes of yellow are provided by rudbeckias and the egg-yolk-coloured daisies of helianthus. Holding court in the centre of the bed is a huge clump of *Persicaria microcephala* 'Red Dragon', a fast-growing perennial with triangular, purple leaves.

TIP
Many exotics have a tendency to spread quickly, but don't be afraid to control growth by removing leaves or stems that have outgrown their space.

Tonal change

A gradual shift in warm shades provides an invigorating spectacle.

Time to plant: Spring or autumn.

This bold border is testament to the owner's skill at combining flowers. The dark shades of red gradually change to orange and yellow, a tonal shift that is harmonious, resulting in a colour scheme that is invigorating, exhilarating and magnificent.

Fiery *Crocosmia* 'Lucifer' rubs shoulders with a crimson helenium, above the flat plates of bright red *Achillea millefolium* 'Fanal'. Stout spikes of red-hot poker, *Kniphofia* 'Toffee Nosed', which start off soft orange and fade to cream, provide vertical interest at the back of the border. In front, an orangey-brown helenium joins a mass of terracotta, pinkish-red and yellow achilleas.

To ensure that the plants are displayed at their best, the fence has been painted a dark, recessive shade of blue. The trick is highly effective. The eye is instantly drawn to the flowers, which are presented in stark relief to the boundary.

TIP
To add texture and movement to a border, dot swishy ornamental grasses like *Stipa tenuissima* between plants.

Variety is the spice of life

Mark the seasons with plants that give instant impact.

Time to plant: Late spring.

Perhaps the easiest way to give your garden a pick-me-up without having to dig deep into your pockets to get it redesigned, is to make the most of seasonal plants.

Head to your nearest garden centre at any time of year and you'll find the shelves groaning with cheap and cheerful annuals. These will add a splash of colour to your garden for weeks or sometimes even months.

These plants can be used to plug gaps in borders, to create hanging baskets or displays to give patio containers a lift. For a great combination, try *Ipomoea batatas* 'Blackie' with *Euphorbia hypericifolia* 'Diamond Frost'. The dark purple, large-lobed leaves of 'Blackie' trail abundantly and are the perfect foil for the clouds of tiny white flowers that adorn the wiry stems of the euphorbia.

TIPS

The euphorbia will flower its socks off in sun or part shade. Keep the container well watered for a long-lasting display.

Brighten up gravel

Use container-grown bulbs to transform a sea of gravel.

Time to plant: Spring.

A sea of gravel can look quite stark, but it is easy to transform with bulbs. Rather than planting them in the soil under the gravel, buy container-grown bulbs in bud and plunge them into the gravel where they are to flower.

This is easy to do and means you can change the display to mark the seasons. Simply scoop back some gravel and pop the container into the hole, making sure you cover it up well so no bits of plastic are visible. For a natural-looking display, dot the bulbs around and avoid serried rows.

So why not plant bulbs directly into the soil beneath the gravel in autumn? Well, you could, but in most gardens gravel is laid in a thick layer over landscape fabric. Planting into the soil beneath would mean a lot of excavation and you would have to cut holes in the fabric, which would defeat the object of laying it in the first place. Soil would get mixed in with the gravel, and weeds could also push their way up through the holes.

TIPS
After they have finished flowering, remove the pots of bulbs from the gravel. Replace with pots of short alliums in early summer, followed by eucomis and then nerines in the autumn.

Green wall

Vertical panels of plants.

Time to plant: Spring or autumn.

A novel way of breaking up the uniformity of a vertical surface is to make a green wall. Ideal for those living in flats, these can be placed on any wall and can be used to grow hardy succulents, bedding plants, herbs or even small vegetables, such as lettuces, radishes and spring onions.

In the past this has always been a DIY job for talented garden designers, but there are now several systems available that make it easy for anyone to have a green wall.

One such system consists of a rectangular metal tray that is attached to the wall with a hook. Polystyrene trays are then filled with water-retentive compost and planted up horizontally. These are inserted into the frame and a wire mesh grid put on the front to stop the plants falling out.

TIPS
You will need an outdoor tap, as green walls need to be watered by an automatic irrigation system. If installing a green wall high up, ensure it is firmly locked in place and can't be accidentally dislodged.

Cracking up

Plant up tiny gaps at ground level.

Time to plant: Spring or autumn.

The gaps between paving slabs offer lots of planting opportunities. Whether on a patio, along a path or up some steps, these narrow strips can be filled with many fabulous plants. Prepare gaps for planting by removing loose mortar and adding some loam-based compost.

Traditionally these spaces have been planted with ground-hugging herbs that release their scent when trodden under foot, such as Corsican mint (*Mentha requienii*), or mat-forming varieties of thyme. However, there's no reason why you have to stick rigidly to these tried-and-tested plants.

Low-growing plants are best. Grassy thrift, glossy leaved ajuga and houseleeks are ideal, as are several grasses, such as *Briza maxima* or quaking grass, and fluffy white-headed hare's tail, *Lagurus ovatus*. You could even add early interest with crocuses, dwarf irises, snowdrops and other compact spring bulbs.

TIP
Hardy annuals are ideal for gaps in paving – sow seeds in spring where they are to flower. Ferns are great in gaps if you have a path in shade.

The only way is up

Get height into a raised bed

Time to plant: Spring or autumn.

If you think you need a large garden or at least a big patch of bare soil for a sensational border, think again. Even a tiny paved backyard can become a plant-filled paradise.

Despite lacking any soil whatsoever in this paved courtyard, the owner has still managed to grow lots of plants by building a raised bed, filled with a mixture of garden compost and topsoil. Placed against a boundary, it doesn't interfere with access to the courtyard or take up too much space.

Although slim, this raised bed includes a mixture of plants that give a long season of interest. Providing height at the back is a castor oil plant (*Ricinus communis* 'Carmencita') and purple fennel (*Foeniculum vulgare* 'Purpureum') alongside white-flowered *Nicotiana sylvestris* and cannas. LOwer-growing phormiums and grasses spill over the front of the bed.

TIPS

Plants in raised beds will need pruning and sometimes replacing to ensure they don't take over. If your garden doesn't have solid boundaries, use a cane, willow or reed panel to give privacy and act as a backdrop to planting schemes.

Well-behaved blackberries

Get masses of plump fruit from compact plants.

Time to plant: Any time of year.

Most blackberries are unruly thugs, too wild for growing in a small garden. Their vigorous, spreading habit and stems clad in sharp thorns (which snag your clothes whenever you walk down the garden path), mean you are unlikely to choose to grow them if you're short on space.

However, if you are a lover of these fat, juicy berries, don't despair. Recent breeding work has come to the rescue and there are now several varieties that are perfect for small gardens. Among them is 'Loch Maree', a thornless blackberry that is happy growing in a large pot, so it can be pushed out of the way against a wall or fence. This plant is showier than most, with masses of pink flowers in spring, followed by a heavy crop of delicious fruit from late summer until the middle of autumn.

TIP
'Loch Maree' is perfect in a 15-litre pot. Train the shoots up a 1.8m (6ft) cane and tie in as they grow. Water and feed regularly with a high-potash fertiliser to ensure a heavy crop. Cut fruited shoots to the ground in autumn.

Doubling up

Nasturtiums give pumpkins a floral pick-me-up.

Time to sow: Sow nasturtiums outdoors in late spring or early summer. Sow pumpkin seeds indoors in early spring for planting out in May.

Pumpkins, squashes and courgettes are perfect in pots, but the plants are a little dull and take up too much space to warrant growing them on their own. Of course, the end crop is delicious, but these plants take several months to reach maturity and all you have to look at during this time are some massive, but not particularly pretty, leaves.

This failing is easy to remedy. Simply sow a few trailing nasturtium seeds in the container when you plant out the pumpkin or courgette. The nasturtiums will grow quickly, tumbling down the sides of the pot or climbing through the pumpkin plant, using its stems as supports.

As well as creating a striking show of colour, nasturtium flowers are also edible. They have a peppery taste and are perfect for brightening up a summer salad.

TIPS
Pumpkins are good in a redundant corner, where you won't walk on the trailing stems. Grow in a 25-litre pot and keep well watered. If the fruit sounds hollow when you tap it, it should be ready for harvesting.

Portable herb garden

Herbs in pots make a moveable feast.

Time to plant: Spring to autumn.

Everybody who is passionate about cooking dreams of having an extensive herb garden full to the brim with tasty leaves. These can be used to add flavour to a recipe or the finishing touches to the perfect meal.

However, very few of us have enough room for a dedicated herb garden. So should you deprive yourself of these valuable plants? Absolutely not. Most culinary herbs can be grown in containers, making them perfect for anyone with a roof garden, courtyard or patio – or even just a windowsill.

Aim to make a real feature of your herbs by growing them in a variety of pots – choose different shapes, sizes, colours and materials. Arrange them in groups and change the display when a plant runs out of steam or whenever the mood takes you. For year-round interest, and to ensure there is always something to pick, grow a combination of long-lasting herbs, such as thyme, rosemary and mint, along with annuals and short-lived options, such as parsley, basil and coriander.

TIPS

Allow the herbs to flower if you want to attract bees and butterflies. Most herbs will do well in multi-purpose compost, but grow thymes in gritty John Innes No.2.

Bags of potatoes

Enjoy your own fresh spuds.

Time to plant: February to March.

Digging up potatoes is the gardening equivalent of striking gold. One minute you have bare soil, then plunge in a fork, prise upwards and, eureka, you'll uncover masses of precious potatoes.

If you want to experience this thrill, you don't need a dedicated kitchen garden or allotment. Potatoes are perfect for growing on the patio in large pots or sacks lined with plastic. You can even buy special potato growing bags, which are designed to look good, so you don't need to hide them. They also have handles so you can move them to another part of the garden if they are getting in the way.

To grow potatoes in a pot or sack, space three tubers on a 10cm (4in) layer of compost and cover with a similar amount. As the foliage grows, earth up regularly with more compost, stopping when you are about 10cm (4in) from the top. Don't expect a huge harvest, but even the contents of a single pot should provide you with enough potatoes for several meals.

TIPS
Water regularly and don't let the compost dry out. Harvest when the foliage starts to die back. Make sure you harvest all the tubers before digging the spent compost into your garden, otherwise you'll have potatoes popping up everywhere.

Bountiful beds

A compact space for growing edibles.

Time to plant: Mainly in the spring, but possible all year round.

A raised bed is a bit like a giant container and is an ideal way to grow lots of vegetables in a compact space. Essentially a square or rectangular frame filled with a compost mix, a raised bed can be made from a pile of old bricks, untreated railway sleepers or newly bought timber. Alternatively, you can buy a kit, which is really simple to put together.

Although they can be made up to waist height, a 90cm (3ft) square bed with sides about 20cm (8in) high is ideal for most gardens. Grow plants in rows or create an ornamental effect. Try growing vegetables such as cabbages, courgettes, salads, aubergines, cherry tomatoes, dwarf beans, broad beans and runner beans. You can also pop in some herbs.

Place your bed in a sunny, sheltered spot and protect from slugs and snails by sticking a band of copper tape around the outside. To ensure plants thrive, keep the bed well watered and free of weeds. An ideal compost for raised beds is 50 per cent sterilised topsoil and 50 per cent multi-purpose compost, with a few handfuls of horticultural grit.

TIP
To make the best use of raised beds, replace spent crops with new ones immediately.

Salad tray

Save pounds by growing your own salad leaves.

Time to sow: Spring and summer.

Supermarket salad leaves can be expensive, but it's cheap and easy to grow your own. Although many types of traditional containers are ideal for salads, why restrict yourself? It can be great fun to recycle objects that were going to be thrown away, such as old fruit trays.

Even though wooden fruit trays aren't very large, they provide more than enough room for salad crops. Look out for them with the spare cardboard boxes in supermarkets or left for the refuse collectors to pick up at local markets.

Try sowing a blended mixture of seeds, containing several varieties of lettuces, mustards or oriental leaves, or grow short rows of your favourites. Pick the leaves when they are young on a regular basis to ensure a steady supply for several weeks.

TIPS

If you have room, sow another tray a couple of weeks after the first to provide a succession of pickings. Keep the plants well watered. Place the tray on an outdoor table when you're eating, so guests can pick their own.

Another bite of the cherry

Enjoy sweet cherry tomatoes all summer long.

Time to plant: Sow seeds from February to April. Grow under glass, or plant outside from late May, when all risk of frost has passed.

If you were to compare cherry tomatoes to an item of jewellery, it would have to be to a pair of garish, fun, Carmen Miranda-style earrings. Hanging in large clusters, the bright red, glossy baubles are borne prolifically, where they tempt you to pick them whenever you step foot outside the back door.

All tomatoes can be grown in small gardens, from chunky beefsteaks to weird and wonderful heritage varieties, but if you can only grow one type, choose one that will reward you with these diminutive fruit. Why? Because the plants will crop their socks off from mid-summer until the end of September, really earning their keep.

And that is, of course, the golden rule for any crop you grow in a small garden.

Either plant them individually in large pots or grow several together in a grow bag. They'll need to be trained up canes about 1.8m (6ft) high and love a sunny spot. Keep them out of the way by pushing them up against the house or next to a fence. Even smaller and more prolific than cherry tomatoes are the marble-sized fruits of 'Hundreds and Thousands', which can produce up to 2,000 tomatoes on a single plant.

TIP
Pinch out the main shoot when it reaches the top of the cane. You can also nip out side-shoots to keep plants within bounds. Turn excess fruits into tomato sauce and freeze it for use later.

Strawberry tower

Masses of delicious and fragrant red berries in summer.

Time to plant: Bare-rooted runners from July to September. Pot-grown plants at any time.

Strawberries are our favourite summer fruit, whether served with champagne, ice cream or simply swimming in a pool of cream. They are also simple to grow – after planting, all you really have to do is water and feed them to enjoy a heavy crop of plump berries.

Although a single plant will reward you with enough fruit for a few meals, several plants will provide you with berries for many weeks. A great way to squeeze them into a small garden is to grow them in a tower of three different-sized pots. Strawberry plants will produce many new runners each summer. Unwanted runners can be cut away, or you could root some into small pots and plant them up later.

Start with a 45cm (18in) pot fill with compost, then sit a 25cm (10in) pot on top. Fill this with more compost and finish with a 13cm (5in) pot. Now put four plants around the edge of the lowest pot, three in the middle pot, and finish with a single plant in the top. Place the strawberry tower in a sunny spot and water the pots regularly, especially during dry, sunny weather.

TIP
Feed the plants weekly with a liquid tomato fertiliser when flowers appear. After harvesting, cut back any tatty foliage.

Full of beans

Variegated sage makes an attractive foil for purple-podded beans.

Time to plant: Sow bean seeds indoors between March and April. Plant out with sage in May.

They may be short, but dwarf French beans make up for their slight stature by producing armfuls of slender pods from summer into autumn. There are lots of great varieties available, but if you only have room for one, go for something eyecatching. Don't settle for typical green beans when you can have the glossy dark pods of 'Purple Queen'. And they'll look even better above a mat of variegated sage (*Salvia officinalis* 'Tricolor').

Start the beans off on a windowsill or in a greenhouse in early spring. Sow the seeds 4cm (1½in) deep, into 7.5cm (3in) pots. Water regularly and transplant into a 30cm (12in) diameter container, filled with free-draining, soil-based compost in May.

TIP
For the best beans, harvest when young, picking twice a week. Keep the sage compact and productive by nipping out the shoots.

Square-foot gardening

Grow nine crops in a small square bed.

Time to plant: Sow seeds and plant out ready-grown plants in late spring.

This crop of onions is ready for harvesting in a square-foot garden, a space-saving technique for raising edibles on the smallest patio, balcony or roof garden.

Construct a simple raised bed by nailing four lengths of timber together. A 90cm x 90cm (3ft x 3ft) structure will allow you to grow nine different vegetables. Fill the bed with compost and divide it into squares. You can do this roughly by hammering short nails around the outside and running strings across to make a grid.

Sow a different crop into each square. Suitably low-growing or compact options include onions, spring onions, peppers, an aubergine, basil, chard, strawberries, chillies, dwarf beans, rocket and beetroot.

Either sow your chosen crops straight into the soil or plant out ready-grown crops in late spring after all danger of frost has passed.

TIPS
After sowing, cover with chicken wire until the seedlings appear. Thin out the seedlings when necessary. To get the most out of the bed, plant it up again in autumn for crops to pick over winter.

Give a fig

Plant in a pot for handsome leaves and succulent fruit.

Time to plant: Any time of year.

This fig, *Ficus carica* 'Violetta', is worth growing simply for its lovely, large, deeply lobed leaves. But it has the added bonus of deliciously sweet fruits, blushed red and produced in abundance. What's more, it's one of the hardiest varieties, surviving temperatures down to -20°C.

If planted in the ground and left to their own devices, fig trees grow rampantly and produce little fruit. But when grown in pots with their roots restricted, they produce lots of fat, juicy figs.

Grow a fig in a 45cm (17in) pot filled with a loam-based compost – John Innes No.3 is ideal. When the fruits are growing, feed weekly with a liquid tomato food. To prevent plants sprawling or becoming too tall, pinch back the shoots. Apart from keeping plants compact, this will result in a flush of new branches that will carry fruit.

TIP
Figs need lots of nutrients, so mix some controlled-release fertiliser granules into the top layer of compost in early spring.

Gooseberry lollipops

Juicy summer fruits on a single stem.

Time to plant: Container-grown plants all year round; bare-rooted plants from November to March.

Gooseberries are often grown as large bushes in open ground. However, in a small garden the best way to grow them is as a half-standard (with a clear stem and a lollipop-shaped head) in a large pot. Although more compact, you'll still get a good crop of melt-in-the-mouth berries.

Raising the cropping head means the plant takes up less space on the ground, while providing some vertical interest. Don't worry, you don't need to carry out any fancy pruning techniques to grow a half-standard, as ready-trained plants are available to buy from nurseries.

Excellent gooseberry varieties include 'Invicta', which gives a heavy crop of pale green berries from mid-summer, and 'Remarka', whose dark red fruits have smooth skins. 'Hinnonmaki Yellow' produces large, yellow fruits.

To make more use of the container, underplant the gooseberry with herbs, such as sage, parsley and basil, or allow alpine strawberries to cascade down the sides.

TIP

Gooseberries need plenty of water, especially in dry weather. Prune after harvesting to maintain an attractive shape and encourage a good crop next year. Cut back the side branches, not the main shoots, to five leaves. Pull off any suckers from the base in summer.

Trained to perfection

An easy way to grow fruit against a fence or wall.

Time to plant: Bare-rooted plants from November to March.

If you have room, it's great to grow fruit as free-standing trees or bushes. But if space is limited, you can restrict their growth by training them as cordons. You'll still get plenty of fruit and they'll brighten up a boring fence or wall.

Usually planted at a 45-degree angle (although they can be grown bolt upright), cordons should be planted against a bamboo cane, secured to wire supports attached to a fence or wall. Three parallel wires, 60cm (2ft) apart, held between straining bolts or secured to vine eyes would be ideal.

Many types of fruit can be grown as cordons, including apples, pears and gooseberries, as well as whitecurrants and redcurrants, such as 'Rovada', shown here. Most need a south- or south-west facing wall to thrive, but this redcurrant can be grown against a shady, north-facing wall, although the flavour of its fruits won't be quite as good.

TIP

To get the best crop, prune a redcurrant in winter by shortening the main shoot to leave 15cm (6in) of the previous season's growth and reduce the side shoots to two buds. In summer, reduce side-shoots to five leaves. When the main shoot has reached its allotted height, prune back each winter to leave one bud of last season's growth.

Small but perfectly formed

Choose a compact shed that won't become an eyesore.

Time to do it: Any time of year.

In a small garden, the average 1.8m x 1.2m (6ft x 4ft) shed would stand out like a monstrous carbuncle. Unless you are a complete shed-a-holic who needs to worship daily in a cathedral of softwood timber, something a little more compact might be more suitable.

The answer for anyone who wants the convenience of a shed but doesn't want it to encroach on their growing space, is to install a lean-to shed. Measuring about 1m (3.3ft) high by 2m (6.5ft) wide by 45cm (18in) deep, there's not enough room for you to get inside to do the crossword or listen to the radio, but there's more than enough space for your tools and all the other bits and pieces you need to maintain the garden.

Alternatively, if you don't have any bulky tools, go for a lean-to tall store instead. These can even be hidden away in a rarely used side passage. Make the most of the limited space by adding hooks for hand tools and pockets for seed storage to the inner walls and door.

TIP
You can squeeze more plants into the garden by covering the shed with a green roof. Cover with pond liner to prevent moisture seeping into the shed, add a box frame around the edge and fill with compost into which you can put plants such as sedums and alpines (see p154).

A bench for all seasons

A clever storage device with several uses.

Time to do it: Any time of year.

Does your garden need reclaiming from a jumble of old pots, kids' toys and abandoned hand tools? If the answer is yes, build a brick storage bench and you'll have an attractive garden seat that doubles up as a hidden waterproof cupboard.

The bench can be sited anywhere in the garden, but a sunny spot is best. Put it where you can sit and catch some rays – by the edge of a patio or next to a deck would be ideal. To be useful, it needs to be about 150cm (58in) in length and about 50cm (20in) wide. If you have a tricky corner that needs a seat, try making a customised L-shaped bench.

Choose bricks that match the colour of your house wall or paving, building it five or six courses high. Then make a waterproof lid, which doubles as a seat, from marine ply and strips of pine. Give it a coat of exterior paint and it'll be a practical and attractive feature.

TIP
A bench makes a great place to display a collection of plants. If you don't think your DIY skills can stretch to making one, you can buy various funky storage seats (with removable tops) that are great as outdoor dining chairs.

Free water supply

Save water with a slimline water butt.

Time to do it: Any time of year.

Many water butts are big and bulky, but slimline models are also available that will sit tightly against the house wall. These are ideal for the most compact of places, such as narrow side passages. In fact, a location like this is ideal, unless you are happy for a butt to be in full view or rob you of valuable growing space.

Typical slender butts can store 100 litres of water and measure about 1m (3.3ft) tall by 40cm (16in) wide. Simple to fit, they can be attached to the downpipe of gutters and can fill up overnight if you get heavy rain.

You could also fix a water butt to a greenhouse, shed, outdoor office or any other garden building with gutters and a downpipe. Do make sure you've considered where the overflow will run off to, especially if the butt is against a wooden fence or shed wall.

TIPS
Place the butt on a stand so you can get a watering can comfortably under the tap. Don't use water from the butt for watering seedlings as it may contain bacteria that could kill them.

Stylish storage solutions

Outdoor cupboards that echo those indoors.

Time to do it: Any time of year.

In many modern gardens there is a strong physical and visual link between the house and garden. The only barrier that separates the two may be a sliding glass door. This allows the owner to create a garden where there is a seamless flow from inside to out, using similar colours and materials.

All well and good until you need to find places to hide away modern necessities such as wheelie bins or lawnmowers.

In a contemporary garden like this, a traditional shed of any size would look completely out of place. The solution: cupboards that mimic those found in the kitchen. Made from sustainably sourced hardwood timber, such as oak, balau or western red cedar, these will last a long time and weather well without being treated with preservatives.

TIP
To soften the look of the cupboards you could plant the top up with fast-spreading mind-your-own-business. Keep it neatly trimmed, otherwise a sleek effect will start to look a bit ragged.

Watering made easy

Save time by setting up an automatic irrigation system.

Time to do it: Any time of year.

Short on time? Then install a micro-irrigation system to keep all your plants in pots well watered. You can design your own system, buying separate parts and building it from scratch. However, fitting it together can be complicated, unless you are a whizz at DIY or have an aptitude for following instructions.

Fortunately, there are lots of boxed kits available that contain everything you need and are easy to set up. You simply take them out of the box and they are more or less ready to go.

Most irrigation systems work in the same way. Water is delivered to the plants through tiny nozzles that sit at the end of long, thin, spaghetti-like pipes connected to a longer hosepipe. This is then attached to a computerised timing device plugged into an outdoor tap. Set the timer to come on for a short period of time in the morning and in the evening. You can even run it from a water butt by adding a submersible pump.

TIP
If you are planting new, permanent containers, thread the thin tubing through the drainage hole in the base. It can be run inside the pot and sit on top lots of unsightly tubes showing.

Top it off in style

A decorative layer looks attractive and is good for plants.

Time to do it: Ideally in spring, but any time.

There's often enough room in a large pot to grow several plants, ensuring you get the maximum amount of interest out of the available space. But this isn't usually possible in a small pot for long. Does that mean you have to stare at bare compost? No, of course not. Simply spread a layer of decorative material over the surface, which will add texture and interest to your garden.

Natural materials look best, such as pine cones, sea shells, pebbles or stones. Avoid crushed CDs and brightly coloured pieces of glass – these are the mulch equivalent of a loud Hawaiian shirt.

Apart from embellishing your pots, mulches have a practical purpose. A thick layer of material will hinder the germination of weed seeds, while also helping to retain moisture, so you don't need to water as often. Top up the mulch whenever necessary.

TIP
Covering the compost means you can't see if it is drying out. Regularly check if you need to water by removing some of the mulch.

A vintage collection

Use old junk to create a bright, colourful and individual garden.

Time to do it: Any time of year.

Pots are more visible in a small garden and it's difficult to hide ugly plastic ones from view. Rather than camouflaging those you are ashamed of, try growing some plants in recycled containers. They look bright and you can display your plants proudly.

Industrial food tins and olive oil tins can be acquired from local restaurants and delicatessens. Or check out supermarkets or ethnic food stores for tins with attractive designs that would make an eye-catching feature. Aim to get a selection in different shapes and sizes so you can make an interesting display.

Before potting them up, clean them out well and drill some drainage holes in the bottom. Then simply plant them up with vegetables, herbs or flowers.

TIPS
Jazz up a plain tin with a coat of paint. You don't need to stick to recycled food containers – try an metal watering can, bucket or colander, a teapot or even a cup and saucer. Remember that plants in small pots will need watering more often than those in larger containers.

Condition your soil

Turn dead leaves into valuable compost.

Time to do it: Autumn.

Fallen leaves may be a pain, but resist the temptation to consign them to the wheelie bin. Instead, turn leaves from deciduous trees and shrubs into useful leaf mould. This crumbly compost can be spread over borders as a weed-suppressing mulch or dug in to improve the soil.

If you have a spare corner, you can store fallen leaves in a cage made from chicken wire. But if space is tight, simply rake them up and put them in a black bin bag. If the leaves are dry, sprinkle them with water and give the bag a shake before tying a knot in the top. Then pierce the sides and bottom a few times to allow excess water to drain out.

Store the bags of leaves in a shaded spot (behind a shed is perfect). Open them next autumn and you'll find a bulky mulch, or leave for two years and you'll have a finer material that makes a wonderful soil conditioner.

TIPS
Most leaves from deciduous trees will rot quickly, but evergreen leaves will take longer – use them sparingly and shred first before adding to the leaf bin. Jute sacks are a more attractive, but expensive, alternative to bin bags.

Sculptural bird bath

Keep birds happy with an arty bath.

Time to do it: Any time of year.

Everybody knows birds are good for the garden. Not only are they great to watch, but many of them will devour smaller creatures that we consider pests, such as caterpillars, aphids, slugs and snails.

Attracting them makes sense, but the problem with many of the items that you need to entice them to the garden is that they simply don't look good. Bird baths are a good case in point; some can be formal, ornate or twee, and in a garden the size of a postage stamp they are going to draw the eye like a beacon.

However, this mosaic bird bath is a beautiful addition to the garden. Apart from being practical, it is highly sculptural, adding an artistic statement to the branches of a tree. You can easily make a bird bath like this by pressing mosaic tiles or pieces of broken crockery on to a terracotta bowl covered with tiling mortar. Drill three holes to thread some wire through and hang from a branch.

TIP
Check out secondhand or junk shops for attractive items that might make an interesting bird bath.

Room to grow

How to choose the perfect greenhouse for a small garden.

Time to do it: Any time of year.

Greenhouses are brilliant if you have lots of plants that need protecting over winter, want to start vegetables off early, or need room to raise seedlings.

To choose the right model, decide what you want to spend and also how much room you can afford to give to it without losing too much outdoor space. Greenhouses with vents in the roof and louvred vents on the side are best, as they allow much better control over air flow.

When fitting it out, buy a heater and add a light so you can potter about after dark in busy spring and autumn evenings. Freestanding, tiered staging units and shelves that can be attached to the internal glazing bars will help you keep everything neat and tidy.

In the past, greenhouse floors were largely soil, which allowed gardeners to plant straight into it. It's far more versatile to have a hard floor – in summer you can cool down the air temperature by splashing it with water every morning; in winter you can stack the floor with pots of tender plants.

TIPS

Put your greenhouse in a light, sheltered spot. Use the space carefully – place large plants on the ground, while seedlings, smaller plants and those that need lots of light should be grown on the upper tiers of staging.

Pots for all seasons

Use seasonal bulbs for a splash of colour.

Time to plant: Spring bulbs, plant in autumn; summer bulbs in spring; autumn bulbs in late summer.

Tulips, daffodils and scented hyacinths are ideal for growing in pots. Even if you have a little more than a patio, they're a great way to inject their garden with some colour in spring. Plant up several pots, each with a different variety, then arrange in groups to create an eye-catching spectacle.

But what do you do when the flowers start to fade? Well, rather than wait for next spring, fill some more pots with bulbs that will light up the garden at other times of the year, too.

Plant lilies, cannas, agapanthus, pineapple lilies and zantedeschias for their exotic summer flowers. Follow these with cyclamen, *Amaryllis belladonna*, colchicums and autumn-flowering crocus to finish up with a striking show of late colour. Cheap and cheerful bedding plants will add interest to pots while you're waiting for the bulbs to grow and flower.

TIPS

Some bulbs, including pineapple lilies and cannas, are not fully hardy and need to be moved to a frost-free place over winter. Deadhead flowers as they start to fade to keep displays looking neat. Water regularly when in growth.

Turf love

Keeping your green space in great shape.

Time to do it: Autumn.

When you've only got a small lawn, be prepared to make annual repairs to keep it in good shape. Damage from foot traffic, pets and children playing will be concentrated into one small area, taking a heavy toll. And because the lawn is tiny, problem areas are also going to be more noticeable.

Bare patches are among the most common problems that you will need to remedy. Using a half-moon cutter or sharp spade, slice out the damaged or dead turf in a neat rectangle or square. Break up the underlying soil slightly with a hand fork.

Buy enough new turf to fill the gap and use the same fork to lightly loosen the soil underneath. Cut the turf to size and firm it down, ensuring that the edges fit together perfectly and leaves neither a gap nor a ridge.

TIP
Ensure you have the right turf for your requirements. Hard-wearing, domestic turf, mainly containing dwarf perennial rye grass, makes a great family lawn. Fine turf, comprising bents, fescues and smooth-stalked meadow grass, looks great, as long as you don't walk on it too often.

Looking peachy

A delicious addition to any garden.

Time to plant: Bare-rooted plants from November to March.

The only place you used to be able to find apricots, peaches and nectarines was in tins, where the thin slivers of fruit swam in heavy syrup. Today, fresh fruit is widely available in shops, but nothing compares to picking your own fruit that has spent time ripening under the sun.

A free-standing tree will supply you with copious fruit, but when space is scarce you will need to restrict its growth by training it against a sunny fence as a fan – with diagonally trained branches – or with horizontally trained branches.

Apart from providing lots of succulent fruit, these desirable plants will give a dull fence or patch of wall a facelift. Among the best varieties to grow are peach 'Peregrine', apricot 'Flavorcot' and nectarine 'Lord Napier', all of which will produce a reliable crop in our climate.

TIP
Before planting, attach some parallel training wires to your fence. Stretch medium-gauge galvanised wires between restraining bolts secured to the fence uprights. Space the wires every 30cm (12in), measuring from the ground upwards.

Create a buzz

Turn a small garden into a wildlife sanctuary.

Time to do it: Any time of year.

Garden wildlife may be fascinating to watch, but there's a more practical reason for turning your outdoor space into a miniature nature reserve. Birds, amphibians, small mammals and some insects have a ravenous appetite for many creatures that we consider pests so they'll help to keep your plants bug-free, and you'll have less need to reach for chemical pesticides to control them.

A bug box is one of the easiest ways to attract pest-eating insects to your garden. Consisting of an open wooden frame, it is stuffed full of different materials, such as bits of cane, twigs, bark and lengths of stem from plants like buddleia and cow parsley. This provides lots of nooks and crannies for spiders, ladybirds, lacewings and even solitary bees to hibernate in over winter.

TIP
Hang the box from the boughs of a tree or fix it to a shed or fence. You can buy ready-made boxes or make your own.

The height of interest

A rustic obelisk lifts a border.

Time to do it: Spring.

No matter how many plants you've managed to squeeze into it, a border that's all on the same level will look just a little dull. An easy way to punctuate a border is to find room for an obelisk.

There are many types of obelisk available, and what you choose depends on your taste and the style of your garden. A rustic support made from willow or lengths of hazel would look perfect in a rural setting. A contemporary obelisk made from timber or wrought iron would look more at home in a city garden.

Rather than planting the obelisk with perennial climbers, try using annuals. You can change the display every year and be more daring. For an exciting spectacle, try an eye-catching combination of *Ipomoea lobata* (often sold as *Mina lobata*) with yellow-flowered canary creeper (*Tropaeolum peregrinum*), which has gorgeous lobed leaves.

TIP
Raise plants in small pots from seed sown in early spring – plant out when all danger of frost has past. Other annual climbers (or plants usually grown as annuals) to try include sweet peas, morning glory and the cup-and-saucer vine, *Cobaea scandens*.

The perfect backdrop

Grow climbers and wall shrubs up vertical surfaces.

Time to do it: Spring or autumn.

Many owners of small gardens focus on planting up their beds and borders but forget about the walls or fences that enclose their space. Left naked, these vertical boundaries tend to stand out like a sore thumb. However, covered with plants they form the perfect backdrop and allow you to squeeze even more plants into a Lilliputian space.

Before planting up the fences in this tiny patio garden, the owner painted the structures with an exterior paint in a mossy shade of green. Painting fences ensures that no bare timber is visible and provides colour 365 days a year. The shade chosen here is ideal, as it recedes into the background and blurs the boundary, making the garden seem bigger.

When planting up fences, go for a selection of self-clinging climbers, edible plants and wall shrubs. Here, an evergreen ivy and passion flower provide interest all year round, while a grapevine provides a leafy scene for many months, plus fruit and autumn colour. Many other fruit can be grown up walls and fences, including figs, cherries, apples, pears, kiwi fruit and plums.

TIP
Wall shrubs need support, so attach training wires to the fence with restraining bolts. If your garden is really small, go for shrubs with a tight, upright habit rather than those that billow out, such as *Euonymus fortunei* Blondy or *Ceanothus* 'Burkwoodii'.

Column of colour

Add interest to dull walls.

Time to do it: Spring.

Boundary walls are perfect places for supporting plants, but many people don't give a second thought to the walls of their house.

But there is no reason why this vertical space should be devoid of plants. There are many ways to transform fairly dull surfaces into something more beautiful, while at the same time gaining more opportunities to grow even more plants.

An easy way to do this is to use a length of rope to secure several pots together, one above the other, so they can be hung from a wall bracket. Alternatively, buy a ready-knotted set of clay hanging pots. The column of pots breaks up the monotony of the plain wall and allows it to become part of the garden, rather than just a backdrop.

TIP
To keep the display interesting all year round, grow seasonal plants in the pots, changing them as they start to fade. Primulas look great in spring and could be followed by begonias, then use cyclamen and pansies over winter.

On the picket line

Bring out the beauty of your pots with a lick of paint.

Time to do it: All year in good weather.

Fences are often seen as purely functional devices to separate your garden from next door's, but they can be so much more than a visual and physical boundary. Painting the fence immediately shows that it is not just a utilitarian structure marking the outer limits of your kingdom, but an integral part of the overall design and planting scheme.

In back gardens, fences are often painted a shade of green, which helps them blend into the background. But in this front garden there is no apology for giving the picket fence a bright coat of blue. Apart from turning a dull old boundary into a colourful feature, it makes the perfect foil for plants in colourful containers, with shades of yellow standing out especially well.

TIP
Before painting a fence, prepare the surface well by removing any stubborn dirt with a scrubbing brush and some soapy water. Always use exterior paint when painting outdoors.

Master of disguise

A quick and easy way to transform an ugly fence.

Time to do it: Any time.

If you inherit a garden with an ugly fence or have a boundary that has seen better days, you might be thinking about replacing it. However, before you go to the expense of a new fence, consider a cheaper option – covering up the eye sore with a willow screen.

Available in panels or rolls of several different heights, these are easy to fix to existing fences using screws, galvanised nails or staples. If you don't have a fence, but want to use a willow screen, simply hammer in upright fencing posts, add horizontal laths, and fix the screening directly to it.

Cut your willow screen to length once it has been fitted – wear gloves as it is held together with sharp wire. If the screen is too high, cut it to size with secateurs. Mark out your cutting line first, though, to ensure you get a straight edge.

TIP
If willow isn't to your taste, you can also buy bamboo, split bamboo, heather or reed screens.

Succulent globe

An unusual take on the traditional hanging basket.

Time to do it: Spring.

Hanging baskets are a great way of raising plants up to eye level, but if you can't face filling them with traditional bedding plants, then try making a succulent globe. An instant attention-grabber, this novel version of a hanging basket is also easy to look after. Once planted, the drought-tolerant echeverias won't need additional watering.

Despite looking like it might be difficult to make, it's surprisingly easy to construct. To start, line two open-sided, wire hanging baskets. Remove some echeverias from their pots and thread them through the liners. When all the gaps have been filled, add lightweight, gritty compost to the baskets. Put a piece of cardboard over one basket, turn it over and place on top of the other. Carefully pull out the cardboard and wire the two baskets securely together.

TIPS

A 50:50 mix of multi-purpose compost and perlite is ideal. Place your succulent globe in a sheltered, sunny spot. These plants are tender, so move the globe to a frost-free place over winter.

Raise the level

Transform an ugly roof into a high-rise home for plants.

Time to do it: Spring or autumn.

Look out of an upstairs window into your garden. If you can see a shed topped with an unsightly carpet of asphalt, why not give it a makeover by building a green roof?

There are many ways of making them, but the concept is more or less the same. First, cover your roof with waterproof material, such as a butyl pond liner, then add a timber frame around the outside. If the shed is large with a pitched roof, build a grid within the frame to prevent the soil from slipping. Add a drainage layer of gravel and top with capillary matting.

Now add your planting mixture – ideally a 50:50 blend of expanded clay pellets, available from garden centres, and John Innes No.3 compost, spread in a 10cm/4in layer). Add low-growing plants, such as sea campion, thyme, chives, heron's bill (*Erodium* x *kolbianum* 'Natasha'), large blue fescue (*Festuca amethystina*) and biting stonecrop (*Sedum acre*).

TIPS

Before you start, make sure your shed is strong enough to support a green roof. The plants should be able to look after themselves, but you may need to water in periods of drought. Deadhead, divide, weed and remove any unwanted, self-seeded plants on a regular basis.

Outdoor art

Give a small garden a decorative focal point.

Time to do it: All year round.

If your garden is so small that you can step outside your back door and almost touch the rear boundary, it's perfect for turning into an outdoor room. A great way to marry your outdoor space with your home is to take the indoors into the garden by using materials, colours or design ideas found in the house.

The side of this shed echoes the walls found indoors, where pictures, mirrors, wallpaper or other decorative devices are displayed to break up an expanse of bare space. Hung on the shed, this artistic wall hanging turns a humdrum structure into a thing of beauty, disguises an ugly surface and gives this tiny plot a focal point. You could make your own from plywood or buy a ready-made design of powder-coated, brushed or mirror-finished stainless steel.

TIP
Paint the fence or structure first in a different colour, so the wall hanging stands out. Use the wall hanging as trellis and train a climber into it.

Pocketful of plants

Contemporary twist on a traditional hanging basket.

Time to make it: Any time of year.

A contemporary alternative to a traditional hanging basket, this lead planter is perfect for bringing a dull wall to life. Its timeless elegance makes it ideal in a formal town garden.

This planter has been hung on a slightly shady wall, where the three conical pockets have been planted with vibrant campanulas. It could be placed on any garden wall or even a fence, and it offers a great opportunity to add greenery to a tricky space. For instance, if you have a north-facing, shady wall, why not plant the pockets up with ferns? Conversely, if your garden roasts in the sun, plant them up with succulents.

Although it could be hung on its own on the wall, it looks better when plants are trained around it to form a leafy frame. If you have a wall that is already cloaked in a climber, consider pruning some of the shoots to make room for the wall planter.

TIP
This planter was made from a sheet of lead, which can be bought in rolls from DIY stores. A rectangle of lead was fixed to marine plywood, then smaller pieces were cut with metal snips to make planting pockets and fixed in place with clout nails.

Scent from heaven

Perfume your garden with a fragrant climber.

Time to plant: Sow seeds into pots in spring. Plant out in late spring.

In a large garden, the intoxicating scent of sweet peas is often lost until you are virtually on top of the plants. Luckily, in a small garden there is no escaping their rich perfume.

There are simply hundreds of varieties of this annual climber, ranging in colour from white to near black, with many two-tone flowers available. Some blooms are small, while others are large with frilly edges. Two of the most reliable scented sweet peas are the old varieties 'Cupani' and 'Painted Lady'.

For best results, grow sweet peas in a sunny spot. Either plant at the foot of a tree or shrub, allowing them to scramble into the branches, or train them up a wigwam of canes, either in the soil or in a pot on the patio.

To really enjoy them, plant them close to where you like to sit out or dine, and breathe in deeply.

TIP
Deadhead fading blooms to encourage plenty of fresh flowers. Regularly tie the stems to supports to prevent the plants flopping or blowing over.

Add zing to your shed

Turn a tired structure into an attractive feature.

Time to do it: Any time of year in good weather.

A grotty old shed is not the prettiest of sights, but even the most ramshackle structure can be refreshed with a little bit of elbow grease and some TLC.

Shed walls cry out for some decoration. A great way to transform them is to steal an idea from inside the house and attach some shelves to the visible outdoor wall. Either cut out holes using a jigsaw and drop pots into them, or simply stand plants directly on top of the shelf.

Like make-up applied to the face, paint can hide a multitude of flaws and a fresh coat will give the shed an instant lift. Greens will help it disappear into the background, while brighter shades will draw your attention to it, making it more of a garden feature. Paint the shelf a vivid or contrasting colour so it catches the eye.

TIPS
Gerberas, busy Lizzies, calceolarias, and other flowering pot plants would look great on the shelf. Don't forget to water the plants regularly.

Secret spaces

Divide up a garden and add interest.

Time to do it: Any time of year.

Garden screens can add privacy, hide something unsightly, or be used as a backdrop for a group of plants. In a small garden they can make a space more interesting by preventing you from seeing the whole garden at once.

A screen is perfect for creating separate areas. Either attach it to the back of the house, if you have a patio garden, or to a wall or fence, at right angles, so it divides up a narrow, rectangular plot.

In a small garden, it's best to choose a screen with an open design, such as woven hazel or decorative metal. There are even screens modelled on Venetian blinds, with slats that can be opened and closed. Although you can see through them, they still visually break up the space. Avoid solid screens, as these make a small plot appear even smaller and deprive your garden of much-needed light.

TIP
Some screens are moveable, allowing you to continually change the look of the garden. Open screens make perfect supports for climbing plants.

Woven willow

Create natural divisions in your garden.

Time to do it: Any time of year, if you buy ready-made structures.

A densely planted border that echoes a traditional cottage garden oozes informal charm. In a small garden, though, such relaxed planting can sometimes appear just a little shambolic.

Although the lavender, achillea, cosmos and other herbaceous perennials in this border are allowed to rub shoulders without restraint, the display is tempered by a decorative woven screen made from wands of willow and hazel.

Its curvaceous shape is perfectly in keeping with the relaxed nature of the planting scheme. Its vertical form introduces a sculptural element and the way it punctuates the bed adds structure to the care-free scene.

When first placed in a bed, a screen will stand out, but as the season progresses it will become an important part of the whole spectacle. The plants will soon weave themselves around it and use it for support.

TIP
Try making a screen yourself with lengths of living willow. These can be planted between mid-January and the end of March and woven together. They will quickly take root and leaves will sprout along the stems.

Wildlife basket

Use flowers to attract useful butterflies and insects.

Time to plant: Spring.

Even if you don't have a proper garden you can still attract wildlife. Simply make good use of your walls and plant up a wildlife hanging basket. It's ideal for those who only have a tiny patio, courtyard, roof space or balcony.

Bees, butterflies and other flying insects love nectar-rich flowers. This hanging basket is planted with an all-pink combination of some of their favourites, such as lavender, nemesias and verbena. Of course, you don't have to stick rigidly to these plants, as there are plenty of others that will entice wildlife. You could also try veronica, hebe, bugle, cornflowers, ageratum, thrift, heather, alyssum, marigolds and thyme.

Attach a bracket to a warm, sunny spot, hang the basket in place and it'll soon become a magnet for wildlife.

TIP
The display will look good for longer if you deadhead the spent flowers. Water the basket regularly, especially during dry weather. Lavender will need pruning to keep it compact.

Social climbers

Ring the changes each year with one or more annual climbers.

Time to plant: Sow seeds in spring. Plant out in early summer.

Climbing plants aren't only suitable for growing in the ground up walls, fences and trellis. Many will romp away in pots to provide a vertical column of summer colour on flat decks and patios.

Annual climbers are perfect for growing this way and among the easiest is morning glory (Ipomoea). This exuberant climber, which comes in a range of forms, shoots upwards speedily and develops masses of side stems that soon cover obelisks or cane wigwams. From early summer to the middle of autumn, plants are smothered in flowers that open for just one day before being replaced by new ones.

There are many varieties worth trying from the *Ipomoea lobata* (often sold as *Mina lobata*) pictured here, to the instantly recognisable 'Heavenly Blue', to tiny red-flowered *Ipomoea quamoclit* 'Cardinal Climber', which also boasts gorgeous finely divided leaves.

TIP
Sow seeds in February or March. Plant outdoors in early summer into a pot filled with a well-drained, gritty compost. Place it in a sunny position.

Ring the changes

An unusual climber will become a talking point.

Time to plant: Spring.

With pendulous flowers that look like a troupe of ballerinas dancing around the stage in pink tutus, *Rhodochiton atrosanguineus* is a choice climber. It can be trained against a fence or wall, or into the branches of a tree.

Rather than always sticking to the tried and tested, predictable climbers, it's rewarding to grow unusual plants. When you've got limited space, every plant has to earn its keep and this exotic-looking specimen is bound to become a talking point.

Sometimes known as purple bells, this native of Mexico has big, heart-shaped leaves. The purple, tube-shaped flowers which have a cap of pink petals above them, appear from summer into autumn.

Strictly a perennial, is frost tender so is usually grown as an annual. It can reach up to 3m (10ft) tall, but rarely gets to these heights unless grown in a sheltered garden in a mild climate.

TIPS
If you want to keep it going from year to year, but you live in a frosty spot, grow it in a container and put it in a sheltered, frost-free place over winter. Other unusual climbers to try in a small garden include *Lophospermum erubescens*, *Eccremocarpus scaber* and *Dicentra scandens*.

Life on the ledge

Make the most of your sills.

Time to plant: Spring.

If you live in a flat or high-rise building, you might be jealous of those below who have a ground-level garden where they can grow all sort of plants. But rather than becoming green with envy over something you don't have, make the most of what room you do have.

Many properties have windowsills that are deep enough for a window box or narrow trough. These containers can be used to grow lots of different plants and will help to transform a boring brick wall. They come in many styles, from rustic to contemporary, and in a variety of materials, including wood, rattan, zinc, plastic and terracotta.

When choosing a window box, go for one that suits you, the exterior of your house and the plants you plan to grow in it. These could be small evergreens for a year-round display, or annuals such as petunias, lobelias and nasturtiums for lively summer colour.

TIP
Make sure the window box is secured to the sill to prevent accidents below, or attach it to metal brackets screwed into the wall. You could even grow compact herbs, fruit and vegetables in a window box.

A touch of the tropics

Light up an old tree with houseplants.

Time to plant: Spring.

Rather than take an axe to a dead tree or stump, why not use it to support brightly coloured bromeliads? These plants will add a tropical touch to the garden and turn an eyesore into an attractive feature.

Usually grown indoors, bromeliads are a large group of plants that originate in tropical rainforests, where they cling to the branches of trees. It is easy to replicate this in the garden by attaching them to a tree during the warm summer months.

To do this, fix small pots to the branches with nails. Position them behind the branch if possible, so you don't immediately see the container. Then simply slip a bromeliad into each holder. For a great look, place several pots along the branches and a few up the trunk of a stump.

TIP
You don't need to stick to a single variety – try several different bromeliads for a colourful splash. Bromeliads are tender, so don't forget to move the plants under cover in autumn.

Thyme out

Let herbs release their sweet scent.

Time to plant: Spring to autumn.

Forming a tight carpet of grey foliage, woolly thyme (*Thymus pseudolanuginosus)* is often grown between paving slabs, where its scent is released as the stems are crushed underfoot. This lovely ground-covering herb only grows to 7cm (3in) tall, but spreads to 1m (39in). The problem with growing it in a compact garden is that it will be trodden on more often and a pretty plant will soon turn into a battered one.

So, how can you enjoy its spicy scent without planting it in the ground? Simple. Make good use of your walls and raise it up to head height by placing pots on an outdoor shelf. Stop as you pass to crush the leaves or breathe in deeply on a warm day, when its essential oils are released by the sun.

TIP

Thymes love good drainage, so grow them in gritty, soil-based compost. Place the plants in full sun. Woolly thyme isn't fully hardy, so bring it indoors if a cold snap is forecast.

Seat in the shade

A great alternative to traditional garden furniture.

Time to do it: All year round in good weather.

Every garden needs a place where you can relax. It's essential if you are going to treat your garden as an outdoor room for dining, chilling out and socialising, rather than just somewhere to grow plants.

There's enough space in most gardens for a table and the odd chair, but sometimes all this furniture can make a compact garden seem even more cramped. If you're forever pushing it out of the way to give you access to the garden, then you need to find an alternative.

A great idea is to build an arbour next to a fence or wall. It means the centre of your garden remains free of furniture, but gives you somewhere shady to escape the rays of the sun.

TIP
Painting your arbour will help it stand up to the weather and last longer. Choose a colour that will suit your garden and your overall planting scheme. Clothe the vertical trelliswork with scented climbers so you can enjoy their delightful perfume.

Moggie mobile

Turn your trees into outdoor art galleries.

Time to do it: All year round.

A classical bust, tasteful figurine or substantial abstract sculpture all have their place, but it's difficult to find a good spot for them when you only have a few square metres to play with. Does that mean you have to avoid any kind of art in the garden? No, but you need to either find compact pieces that can be worked in without dominating or explore clever ways of displaying your works of art.

If you have a tree, why not make use of its branches? These are fantastic for hanging decorations from, whether it's an expensive trinket from a garden show or a simple design you have made yourself by cutting out a shape from tin with a pair of snippers.

Dangling from the branches, decorations can add interest or mystery, and become a talking point for anyone who sets foot in your garden.

TIP
When displaying art in a tree, remember less is more. Too many decorations will result in it looking like a badly dressed Christmas tree. If it's in a shady spot, choose objects made from mirrors or metal, so they bounce light into the shadows.

Eating al fresco

Turn your fresh produce into delicious meals.

Time to do it: Generally spring to autumn.

British summers may be unreliable, but when the sun shines there is nothing better than rolling out the barbecue and cooking up a great meal with family and friends. If you can supply some of the vegetables from your own garden for kebabs or side dishes, and some herbs for garnishes, the meal will be even more of a success.

Tomatoes, chillies, aubergines and peppers all provide a taste of summer, and are easily grown from seed started off on a windowsill or under cover in March/April. Add courgettes, for grilling, to your seedtrays in April/May.

Take care when choosing a barbecue. Large, hi-tech models look great, but they can dominate a small garden if they can't be stored when not in use. So look for ones that can be taken apart or that will fit into your shed to be wheeled out when needed. Small kettle-drum ones or portable designs are ideal in the tiniest spaces, including a balcony, and can be stowed away easily. You can even throw one into the boot of the car if you are going away for the weekend.

TIPS

Keep herbs close at hand for marinades or to sprinkle on to the coals to infuse the air with their aroma. If you can, separate your cooking and eating areas so your guests aren't engulfed by cooking fumes.

A place to play

Keep children happy with a sandpit.

Time to do it: Spring to autumn.

One of the keys to creating a successful family garden is designing a space that works for parents and children alike. Those with heavily stained green fingers may want to fill every nook and cranny with plants, but if you have a family you need to meet children halfway to ensure that they have somewhere to play, and that everyone is happy.

For many young children, a sandpit is the ideal place to play for hours, and it's always possible to fit one into your garden somewhere, however small it may be.

A plastic pit, like this, can be pushed into a corner so it doesn't get in the way. Spilt sand can easily be swept up if it's placed on a hard surface, such as a deck or patio. Although heavy when filled with sand, it can still be moved to another part of the garden by two or more pairs of hands if need be. If plastic isn't to your taste, wooden pits are widely available, including some that double up as a picnic table when covered by the lid.

TIP
If you're a DIY whiz, an alternative to buying a sand pit is to build your own. Those set into decking are particularly clever – when the hatch is closed it is completely hidden away.

Recycled bird scarer

· Prevent birds from eating your crops.

Time to do it: All year round.

Small gardens are just as attractive to hungry birds as large ones, but when your vegetable patch consists of just a tiny raised bed, the damage can be far more devastating. To prevent your seeds, seedlings and developing produce from being eaten, why not make your own bird scarer?

Built from everyday objects found around the home or often consigned to the bin, this scarer adds a fun touch to the garden, while keeping your plants safe. An unwanted wheel from an old bike is attached to a garden cane, while CDs (use those free ones that come with newspapers) have been tied to the spokes with short lengths of twine.

Birds are frightened by the light reflecting from the shiny surface of the discs and by its movement in a breeze.

More 'allotment chic' than 'chi-chi', this DIY scarer is a quick and easy project to make with kids. And, best of all, it actually works.

TIP
Alternative ways to protect your crops from the attention of birds are with a child's windmill or a traditional scarecrow.

Liberate your shed

Turn a dull structure into a den for kids.

Time to do it: Any time in dry weather.

Sheds are essential for storing the equipment needed to keep the garden going. However, their stark, utilitarian looks aren't what you want in a small garden.

If you have an ugly shed, why not turn it into an attractive feature by giving it a makeover? A simple paint job will suffice in most cases, but if you have a family, why not turn it into a den or Wendy house for small children?

Paint the walls a bright colour and stencil on some flowers or the names of your kids. Inside, add a partition so that you have room to store tools, while they have somewhere to play. Of course, sharp tools, pesticides or any other dangerous items will need to be stored elsewhere.

TIP
Squeeze more plants into your garden by topping the shed with a green roof (see page 154). This will help the playhouse blend into the garden and will attract wildlife for your children to watch.

Rain stops play?

Protecting materials from the weather.

Time to do it: Spring to early autumn.

To really make the most of your garden, you need to be able to relax in comfort without worry. Most of us love sitting in the garden with a glass of wine, a picnic, or even a cup of coffee. However, it can be a real chore to lug soft furnishings in and out of the house every morning and evening or when it starts to rain.

To save time and effort, and to ensure that there is always something comfy to flop down on to, you need to pick your materials carefully. You can choose durable, easy-to-clean fabrics that are waterproof, but you may find these are not always to your taste.

A simpler solution is to pick your favourite fabric for cushions, rugs or throws and spray them with a waterproofing spray such as Fabsil, which is available from outdoor clothing and equipment suppliers, or online. Spray the fabric all over and you can unwind propped up by attractive, stylish furnishings that can be left outside whatever the weather. That's one less worry to ruin your down-time!

TIP
Bring even waterproofed fabrics inside over winter or lengthy wet spells, to allow them to dry out properly.

Space-saving hammock

A great place to rest.

Time to do it: Spring to autumn.

Feeling stressed? Then fall back into a hammock and let your troubles melt away. Nothing beats reclining in the sun, and these most traditional of resting places are perfect where you're short of space.

A wooden recliner requires a lot of floor space, not to mention storage space when not in use, but a hammock is a much more compact option.

Hammocks can be suspended between two trees, sturdy fence posts or the poles erected for a shade sail. Just make sure it is firmly attached when you want to put the hammock away, it's simply a case of folding it up and storing it in the corner of the shed until next year.

This hammock is a homemade one, crafted from simple softwood battens painted with exterior paint and tied together with lengths of marine rope, knotted between each slat. Easy!

TIPS

For sweet dreams, remember to tighten the knots! Site the hammock in a lightly shaded spot. In general, you get what you pay for – cheaper hammocks don't last as long as more expensive ones.

Perfect proportions

Choosing furniture for the scale of your garden.

Time to do it: Best in spring to autumn.

A long rectangular table with bench seats is perfect for a family dinner party. But if it were placed on a small patio, it wouldn't leave you enough room to get up and down from the table.

In a small garden, you should choose furniture that is the right scale for your space. Generally, round tables are more versatile, and single chairs that are stackable or foldable take up less room than solid ones.

This simple and intimate bistro-style table and chairs is perfectly suited to its surroundings and doesn't dominate the patio. Made of cast aluminium, the set is easy to clean with a cloth, can be left outside all year round and is light enough to be pushed into a quiet corner when not in use.

TIP
A few extra folding chairs kept in storage are perfect for visiting friends or family. If buying wooden furniture, choose timber that is certificated to prove it comes from a sustainable source.

Sail away

Create cooling shade in a sunny garden.

Time to do it: All year round.

A problem with some small gardens is the absence of shade. Lack of space means you may not have any large trees nearby. Also, if you the plot is south facing or lit by the sun for many hours each day, it can be quite uncomfortable to spend time relaxing or eating outdoors.

An easy way to get respite from the sun is to put up a shade sail. There are many pre-cut sails available, in different sizes and colours, and in triangular or square shapes. If an off-the-shelf sail doesn't fit into your site or suit your garden, you could get one tailor-made to any size or shape.

To protect you from strong sun or sudden rain, choose a sail made from weatherproof, UV-resistant material.

TIP
Sails can be attached to hooks on tall, sturdy fence posts (don't over-tighten them, or it will strain your fence). Alternatively, put up a permanent framework of poles that have been secured into the ground.

Fabulous front garden

Create the perfect place to sit out.

Time to do it: Plant up in spring or autumn.

If you have a north-facing, shady back garden, you might not want to spend time time outside relaxing. The lack of sunlight means it will only be comfortable to sit out on the warmest days, so aim to make the most of any other space you have.

As long as you're not too self-conscious, a pocket-sized front garden can be turned into the perfect place to relax. It gives you a good opportunity to grow the kind of plants that would suffer from lack of light on the other side of the house, too. It's also the perfect way to meet your neighbours and sociable passers-by.

To maximise the available light, don't enclose the garden with large fences or hedges, but choose a low barrier such as a picket fence and surround yourself with plants.

In this tiny front garden, the owners have made the most of the space by training passion flowers and morning glory over the front door. They've broken up the monotony of the walls with baskets of nasturtiums, convolvulus and purple tradescantia. A fuchsia forms a floral backdrop to pansies, nicotiana, miscanthus and sweetcorn.

TIP
If your front garden is paved, grow plants in pots and make the most of all vertical spaces.

Time for tea (lights)

Atmospheric lighting for outdoor dining.

Time to do it: Spring to autumn.

If you want to use your garden in the evening for outdoor dining, you need to think carefully about how you light it. Avoid anything too harsh around eating areas, such as spotlights or floodlights. Instead, go for something subtle and atmospheric to create the perfect mood.

Here's a great way to do it: use tea lights in strategically placed holders or lanterns to shed light on your table. Hang them from the parasol itself to create the most magical effect.

Place tea lights in small jars, secure them with a loop of wire and attach them to short lengths of chain that can be hung from the internal supports of the parasol. For a really twinkly, romantic effect, intermingle the jars with some shiny Christmas-tree baubles.

TIPS

Remember the golden rule with lighting – less is more. To ward off mosquitoes or other biting insects, place citronella tea lights in the jars.

Magical evenings

Turn a pot of lavender into a light display.

Time to do it: All year round.

During the day, a lavender grown in a tapered pot makes an attractive, scented sentry beside the back door. But on a warm summer's evening, when you might want to spend as long as possible in the garden, you can extend its interest with some dainty fairy lights.

All you need to do is sink a piece of trellis which mimics the shape of the pot into the compost. Then secure the lights carefully to the framework. It's simple, but very effective.

Paint the trellis a similar colour to the flowers, so you achieve a purplish glow after dark. The matching tone will also mean the trellis doesn't stand out like a sore thumb when daylight arrives and ensures the pot will remain attractive even after flowering has finished.

TIPS

If possible, place the display against a light-coloured wall. Using fairy lights in pots is a great alternative to placing them in trees. If you have an outdoor socket, use electric exterior lights, if not, choose solar-powered or battery ones.

A taste of the good life

Make outdoor dining at home really special.

Time to do it: Spring to autumn.

Creating an outdoor dining area is difficult when space is scarce, but it's worth the effort so you can do justice to your food.

Whether you grow fruit and vegetables to save money, for the satisfaction of raising a crop from seed, or simply for fun, nothing beats tucking into a meal that contains plants you have grown yourself.

After working hard to create your garden, it's time to enjoy the fruits of your labours. Put your feet up and enjoy a salad of home-grown produce or a long drink perked up with your own strawberries and a sprig of mint. For this summery drink, stir together 1 teaspoon of caster sugar and the juice of 1 lemon. Pour the mix into two glasses, and half-fill them with ice. Top up with lemonade to a centimetre or so below the rim and finish off with a slice of lemon, lots of sliced strawberries, and mint or borage leaves.

TIPS
Place outdoor dining areas away from cooking areas. If you haven't got room for a table and chairs, try some comfy cushions and a rug on the ground.

Time out

Sit back, relax, and feel the grass between your toes.

Time to do it: All year round.

What do you do after you've designed your dream small garden, made the most of every vertical space and crammed every last nook and cranny with plants? The answer is simple: absolutely nothing.

After all your hard work, you've earned the right to take some time out. Simply enjoy the space you've created, whether it's filled to the brim with plants, a minimalist extension to your home, or a family-focused garden with a daisy-strewn lawn – perfect for walking barefoot through on a warm summer's day. (In fact, it's been medically proven that your blood pressure drops when you relax in green spaces.)

Not only will lounging about recharge your batteries, it will also help you make your garden better than ever. Spending time outdoors allows you to look at what you've created and gives you the chance to conjure up ideas and decide what you want to do next.

TIP
Relax and put your feet up with a long, cool drink. You deserve it.

Index

Picture credits

BBC Books and *Gardeners' World Magazine* would like to thank the following for providing photographs. While every effort has been made to trace and acknowledge all photographers, we should like to apologise should there be any errors or omissions.

Torie Chugg p51 (design: Paul Williams), p55 (design: Paul Williams), p71 (design: Paul Williams), p79 (design: Paul Williams), p149 (design: Paul Williams), p153 (design: Paul Williams), p169 (design: Paul Williams), p177; Eric Crichton p5; Sarah Cuttle p9 (design: Robert Myers, The Cadogan Garden, Chelsea Flower Show 2008), p21 (design: Zoe Cain, Jim Buttress VMH and Jocelyn Armitage, The Way Forward Garden, Chelsea Flower Show 2008), p31 (design: Kevin Smith), p39, p45, p57 (design: Martyn Cox), p59 (design: Martyn Cox), p61 (design: Martyn Cox), p105, p117 (design: Martyn Cox), p119 (design: Martyn Cox), p121, p145 (design: Isabella Ljbeccaborowice), p161, p175, p187, p197, p201; Paul Debois p13 (design: Joe Swift), p19 (design: Helen Riches), p29, p47, p91 (design: Helen Riches), p95 (Clare Matthews), p115, p125, p129, p131, p147, p157 (Clare Matthews), p159 (Clare Matthews), p163, p165, p183 (design: Jayne Keeley); Dig Pictures/Freia Turland p91 (design: Bob Purnell), p189 (design: Paul Williams), p193, p195 (design: Clare Matthews), p199, p203 (design: Cinean Mcternan), p205 (Jayne Keeley), p207; Michelle Garrett p25; Neil Hepworth p179 (design: Nick Bailey); Caroline Hughes p11, p15 (design: Helen Riches), p23 (design: Helen Riches), p35, p53 (design: Helen Riches), p69 (design: Helen Riches), p101, p133; Jason Ingram p17, p27 (design: Toby Buckland), p33 (design: Geoffrey Whiten, Real life Garden, Chelsea Flower Show 2008), p37, p41 (design Adam Frost, A Welcome Sight Garden, Chelsea Flower Show 2008), p43 (design: Helen Riches), p63 (design: Carol Klein and Joe Swift), p65 (design: Alys Fowler), p77, p83 (design: Mandy Buckland, Roger Smith, Ian Dexter, Richard York), p93 (design: Jekka McVicar), p97 (design: Nick Williams-Ellis, Dorset Cereals Edible Playground, Hampton Court Flower Show 2008), p99 (design: Toby and Lisa Buckland), p127, p137, p139, p143 (design: Toby and Lisa Buckland), p151 (design: Joe Swift), p155 (design: Joe Swift), p167 (design: Sim Flemons and John Warland, London Wildlife Trust's Future Garden, Hampton Court Flower Show 2008), p171 (design: Lisa Buckland), p209; Lynn Keddie p81; Noel Murphy p185; David Murray p75, p103, p109, p111, p113; Adrian Myers p49, p85, p181; Tim Sandall p67, p73 (design: Adam Pasco), p89, p107, p123, p135, p173; John Trenholm p141 (design: David Gardner), p191

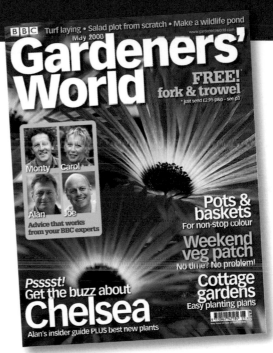